orphan

orphan

JAN HELLER LEVI

ALICE JAMES BOOKS | FARMINGTON, MAINE

10 9 8 7 6 5 4 3 2 1

Alice James Books are published by Alice James Poetry Cooperative, Inc.,
an affiliate of the University of Maine at Farmington.

ALICE JAMES BOOKS
114 PRESCOTT STREET
FARMINGTON, ME 04938
www.alicejamesbooks.org

Library of Congress Cataloging-in-Publication Data
Levi, Jan Heller.
  Orphan / Jan Heller Levi.
    pages cm
  ISBN 978-1-938584-03-9 (pbk.)
  I. Title.
  PS3562.E8877O77 2014
  811'.54--DC23
                        2013029989

Alice James Books gratefully acknowledges support from the University of Maine at
Farmington and the National Endowment for the Arts.

ART WORKS.

COVER ART: Female Figure. Papua New Guinea; Abelam, East Sepik Province. Middle
Sepik. 19TH-20TH century. Wood, paint, H. 42 1/2 IN. (108 CM). The Michael C. Rocke-
feller Memorial Collection, Purchase, Nelson A. Rockefeller Gift, 1962 (1978.412.819).
Photo Credit: Image copyright © The Metropolitan Museum of Art. Image source: Art
Resource, NY

CONTENTS

~

ACKNOWLEDGMENTS

My thanks to the magazines in which versions of these poems
have appeared:

Poetry International: *"the root of bed…,"* *"what do we see…,"*
"the grass is drinking…" and "That's the Way to Travel"
Hanging Loose: "Unlucky" and "Because we like the maps"
Arroyo: "Reading Robert Lowell's 'Skunk Hour' in the 1970s
Barrow Street: "Praise Poem: June Jordan"
Field: "jane, staying, (2)"
The Mom Egg: "Three Songs"
Poets for Living Waters: "The World"

My thanks to Yaddo, where poems are invited to
happen and to the PSC-CUNY Research Award
Program for their grant in support of this book.

And my gratitude and love to Jean Valentine, Anne Marie
Macari, and Joan Larkin, my furies, my friends.

for the Adventurer

&
Jane and Grace

Are there songs rising from the broken sources?

—MURIEL RUKEYSER

Reading Robert Lowell's "Skunk Hour" in the 1970s

As Robert Lowell's car climbed that hill,
we students ran alongside
huffing and puffing.
We wanted to stand
with the master of melancholy
at the top of Blue Hill.
The world had disillusioned us before giving us illusions,
Lowell described that world for us,
the icy rock left for us at the end of the century.

To get there we had to pass by the town fairy
decorating his shop. Here, we were told,
was an example of Lowell's brilliant
compression: the fairy decorator's
fishnet, filled with orange cork,
standing for a whole life
of effeminate affectation, conformity, misery.
The fairy decorator's whole life of conformity
and misery standing for the heterosexual's
whole life of conformity and misery,

so it really wasn't derogatory. Some
managed the arabesque.
Tall boys with blue eyes, mostly.

I remember one particularly, handsome
as the pictures of Lowell when he was young
and driving Jean Stafford's
face into a wall.
Brody could stay up all night
drinking, and debating comma versus semicolon
in Keats, Crane, Dugan, Wright.

I wanted to be with the boys so badly,
watching the red fox stain cover Blue Hill.
But even then I knew I was the fox and I was the stain.

another inventory

there is always more to give up
the wedding drum, the small bronze bell
this bee-leaf and that bee-leaf
the arrow my brother shot through his thumb
and all the lords and ladies in waiting

you require too
my asking tooth
the sundial's gnomon
the flight of stairs knit with the river

you command me to watch:
the smoldering koi leap into the sky's lap
the cicadas drop from the trees, exhausted
from a life of singing

then the walking man—you make him crawl back to his wheelchair

i row and rest
the children rushing past
are kind
they call don't hurry, don't hurry
and leave me behind on this invincible planet

Because we like the maps

we take the trips. The car is ready,
packed. The adventurer waits patiently.
We hug each other, count to 3.

I lift. It's got to be one uninterrupted
lift from wheelchair to feet.
But there's an instant,

midway, when the adventurer
hangs in my arms between rising
and falling—his chest tilts forward,

his butt juts back, his jeans
ride down, his shirt rides up,
his belly dangles in the gap—

it isn't *dignified*. And then we find
the click. It's like we're both holding on
and both letting go—hallelujah—he's

up. On his own two feet. Don't
marry him, some good friends said,
your life will be so *circumscribed*.
At the top of the lift, we've added a kiss.

We'd take the kiss without the lift, but that's
not possible. Maybe our kiss is a gentle

fuck you to anyone who's watching
who thinks our life is less than theirs.
Because we like the maps, we take the trips.

Unlucky

Though there are plants and flowers that are awkward or unlucky… all exert
themselves to accomplish their work, all have the magnificent ambition to
overrun and conquer the surface of the globe by endlessly multiplying
the form of existence which they represent.
—MAETERLINCK, *The Intelligence of the Flowers*

the adventurer, getting out of bed
we've got a don't ask, don't tell policy

the protocol requires patience, arrangements
of limbs and genitals between bed and commode wheelchair

so that mr. johnson doesn't get caught between.
there's something, too, called a "transfer board"

sometimes the adventurer breaks out in a sweat
or makes a choking sound

when he gets stuck
who will we call for help? the police?

imagine.   no, don't. i don't want you imagining
the adventurer naked, his ass

trapped in the gap between mattress
and invacare home-hygiene porto-care, model T-101

i don't want you to imagine him unable to inch forward,
unable to wiggle back, and not knowing whether he'll get

to the toilet in time.   nor do i want you imagining me
and where i stand in this picture

wanting to help, not able to help.   it's genetic

science is getting closer to a cure so people
with his defective gene won't be born

That's the Way to Travel

He was in deep shit is the first line.
The adventurer is writing his 7th novel.
There's a protagonist who uses a wheelchair,

and a murder, and flights of stairs that the protagonist
can't get up or down. Or does he get up and down?
Does he have mysterious powers

that will eventually be revealed?
Few murders have been solved
by a person in a wheelchair.

There was a detective on an old TV series,
but you never saw Ironside stopped outside a door
because his wheelchair was too wide.

It would be good for the reading public
to get to know a character who frequently
can't get into a room, or a store,

or his or her doctor's office. The adventurer's novel
could help change laws, or, at least, attitudes, especially
in the adventurer's native land, where they treat cows

better than cripples. Rimbaud called the bourgeoisie
"the seated." The adventurer is always seated. And like
the bourgeoisie he acquires lots of possessions. His include:

electric wheelchair, 30-pound battery, battery recharger,
adapter plug, surge protector, inflatable cushion,
air pump, spare footrests, spare tires, portable

commode chair, and transfer board. There's also a small,
flexible, plastic-mouthed balloon-like device called a uri-bag.
Lately, the adventurer has been scooting around town,

thinking up ideas for his novel. He gets whomped by sidewalk
potholes, stranded on corners where there isn't a curb cut,
leapt over and leapt around by pedestrians

who think he's a car. He keeps smiling, so he doesn't
look like one of those bitter cripples. Invariably,
someone passing will nod at him—well, not really at him—

but at his wheelchair, grin and say, *That's the way to travel.*
Last night the adventurer and I were talking some non-
bourgeois talk about nomads and gypsies. When

the Europeans tried to destroy Romani culture, they burned
the wheels of the gypsies' wagons. They moved them into concrete
housing projects—running water, electricity. But the gypsies

couldn't stand it. They chopped holes in the roofs so they could still sleep under the sky. You can cut off our wheels, they said, but you can't make us choose ceilings over stars.

Genre

We're watching one of those movies.
I'm lying on the sofa, the adventurer is beside me in his chair.
I've propped up his legs on the needlepoint ottoman.
My mother made it in 1965. (I thought it was ugly until she died.)

Soon after the prognosis/stroke/car wreck/skiing accident,
the one leg dragging behind her. She can't
do things that used to be easy—carry a tea cup

from room to room, take a heavy book off the shelf,
get up from the toilet alone. The adventurer
is beside me in his chair. I get up
to refill our wine. When I come back, the woman's

husband has his arms under her armpits; he
lifts her from the couch to her feet. Like the way
we used to do it when the adventurer could still stand.
In the movie, it looks sad.

Three scenes later, the wheelchair arrives. Note:
all the doors in their apartment are already ADA wide.
Fifteen minutes later, unable to wipe herself,
she wants to die.

The adventurer is beside me in his chair.
No, even our dear friends will say, this isn't about you.
You're different. That woman had nothing to live for.
And the adventurer won't say: the woman loved

music. Loved it. From the moment she comes home
till the husband puts the pillow over her face and holds it down,
no one puts on a record for her to listen to.

What Love Is

To forsake all others.
To float the beloved on your back
from flood to land, to wrench bread
from the beggar's hand, snatch
the oxygen mask from a child's face.
To ransack hospitals and nursing homes
for drugs to ease the beloved's pain,
to stumble down 101 floors, beloved
slung on your back, not stopping
for the other ones in wheelchairs
waiting at the landing doors.

tributary

it is true
i wanted to write a book so holy only god could open it
so only a stone could read it

i wanted to undress an early november
turn back the time on the clock of love

find you
have you take my silence in your hand
your hand, five-petal rose

then came the disintricated woods
the snow-blindness, a degree of dazzling

—i will leave this earth unblooded, blood related to no one—

who will win

two little inuit sisters, bundled in animal skins and furs
chewed with their own teeth,
fighting at the edge of a precipice

in their language it is the same word for "long ago" and "in the future"
what are they saying to each other
let's not let it be *i was always more afraid than you*

Three Songs

My mother lost herself to the burning flu.
My father loved her, he went too.

World thrumming: loveliness rant.
Light shaking on the grass.

My husband wanted children, we had three.
None of them came out of me.
Two grew up, one was born wrong.
Thirty years later, the sickness ate my tongue.

My husband was a healer, but couldn't heal me.
He buried me under a sycamore tree.

ii

The world wears me down with its beating heart.
When it's light outside, I can see the dark.
World thrumming: loveliness rant.
Light shaking on the grass.

I've been carrying a slim bone for a long, long time.
If it's not yours, I guess it's mine.

When my mother died, I swam a river of grief.
The water wrapped me like a coddling sheet.
The cold licked my belly, a lampfish my nose,
and ten little creatures married my toes.

iii

I met a woman in the park downtown.
She was watching her kids on a merry-go-round.
The five-year-old autistic, the three-year-old, Down's.
Those sweet kids went round and round.

Wear me down, world, with your loveliness rant.
Light keeps breaking on the grass.

You're so brave, I went up and said.
I'm not brave, I just love them, she said.

enter the tree

like the gun in the first act
that's required to go off in the last

then the snake

the woman isn't hungry
she doesn't want what he's offering

she just wants out
to see if there are other women around

jane, staying

i've never seen you sleep
i've never seen you wake
now i see both   your crooked honest mouth

so open

I need to tell you why I got angry
they're not giving me time for my writing
I know it's crazy, because I'm not writing
but I need to know I have the time for writing

You Can Tell

In the air, two wobbling stars and a light
under a wing. Invisible wing.

Your story: I'm reading Sam a story.
We come to a picture of a goat.
This goat has absolutely enormous
udders dangling down into the grass.
I ask, Honey, do you think that's a girl
goat or a boy goat? And he says, A girl.
I say, How can you tell? He looks up,
rolls his eyes. Grandma, he says, you can tell
from the way she's smiling.

My story: You have a splendid aura,
the woman on the street says, flickering
a touch on my wrist. Incredible,
she continues, I never do this, I
haven't done this in 15 years, but
do you know you have an incredible
aura? And I never do this, haven't
done this in years, but I stop. I stop, and

she comes close and says it all over again.
She talks quickly, she lights a cigarette,
she's repeating herself, her fingers

are cool and unusually pleasing
on the skin just above my wrist.
You're an artist, she's saying, but they're
out to get you, don't let them get you,
watch out for your thyroid,
your luck's in a knot. You'll have a long life,
live till you're 80, three children
maximum, minimum maybe two.
I tell her there are no children.
No children at all? That's why I said maybe.

I take my hand home, and my instant of believing
and pour myself a glass of ruby-red wine.
I take a sip in honor of my mother,
a woman of valor, her price far beyond
rubies. Okay, no kids, but I'm
going to live till I'm 80. And how
do you know I'm a woman? You can tell
from the way I'm smiling.

jane, staying (2)

the doctors gave you four weeks
now we're going on six
in between, grace stopped eating and went into the stars

you little mandelstam without a revolution
                    but I love this poor earth,
                    because I have not seen another

your hands loop in the air around your window chair,
around your window body

One Little Thing

Father in the car, driving. Daughter in the backseat, being told one
    little thing.
Mother in the passenger seat, smoking, back of her neck very lovely.

Now my mother's needlepointing the thinker into a throw pillow,
taking me into her side of the bed at night,
waking up and arranging her long, droopy breasts into two
    soft mountains.

Now I'm eating lingerie sachets and drinking car wash.
Now she's in the hospital. Going to a PTA meeting. Or rearranging
    hypodermics in the kitchen refrigerator.

My father's in the car, saying one little thing. My mother's checking
    the map.
Or licking green stamps into booklets.
Saving up for the sewing machine I'll never use.

Daughter in the backseat, being told something.
One little thing, it flies through the car—in one window and out

the other—my mother tosses her cigarette out too. Our life.

Mother in the Museum. Leaning over a vitrine called *The Book*.
Father in car, driving. Says something.

Mother turns pages. Daughter in the backseat, off to one side.
Reading. *Give me thy hand, my almost forgotten soul*

That line was a car I got into. Drive and drive.

Sea Captains Carousing in Surinam

oil on bed ticking

Out of great bowls, we drink
Out of long pipes, we see other worlds
We spill, and flail, and scamper

We pat one another's head,
jaunty dance in three-cornered hats,
tap each other with flags, pour forgetfulness

into one another's ears
We overtip chairs
Drop scraps to mangy dogs

One of us vomits into another's pocket

At a large round table we raise glasses,
clap one another on the back
At a smaller table two of us play cards and a third helps one of us cheat

This is what we are
This is what we came for

From the kitchen bar, a naked brown man extends a large bowl

The one of us in the back retching by the door
and trying to leave is the painter

The World

—after Milosz

There—where you see a gradual
decline, beside a raggedy field, mostly dirt,
where new apartment houses will soon be built—
children are walking home from school.

Light beats down from a strict, cloudless sky.
The girls cradle their books in their arms.
The boys trudge ahead like little men,
pretending they have no worries.

When the last child reaches the bottom of the hill,
a low branch of a maple is bobbing.
One of the children, now closer to home,
has torn a leaf from it

to hear the sound the world makes
when we interfere with it.

Thinking about Communism in Fontaine-de-Vaucluse, Source of the Noisy and Emerald-Green Sorgue, Where Petrarch Wrote the Sonnets to Laura and Later Renounced Them

Strange how the din mimics silence.
This is our life of opposites. If I don't stop
listening to the Appassionata, Lenin said,
I won't be able to finish the revolution.
A few were spared, many drowned.

Counting the numbers one way or the other
is the work of the socially-engaged historian.
Not changing our minds about who did what to whom
is the job of the rest of us.
Strange how the din mimics silence.

Before The Call

Not listening but not
not listening to Brahms.
Some clouds churning into larger dark clouds.
The storm cloud of the 19th century, Ruskin called it,
as it passed over, and into his brain.
The average life of a cloud is ten minutes.

In 1877, Ruskin saw Whistler's *Falling Rocket*.
The great art critic had seen and heard
of cockney impudence before, but never
expected a coxcomb to ask two hundred guineas
for flinging a pot of paint in the public's face.
The coxcomb sued for libel. Ruskin didn't make it
to the trial. His century was sputtering out,
the doctors called it brain fever.

Tragedy in one century is learning experience
in another. Anna Karenina going
under that train. Whistler winning the lawsuit,
but going bankrupt. Lizzie Borden going free
because how could a jury convict an orphan?
Ruskin, doddering and drifting, like a cloud,
further and further into madness.

Is it weather
or leaf or cloud beauty, or is it habit
that keeps us climbing and subsiding,
like Brahm's 1891 *Quintet for Clarinet
and Strings in B Minor*, which I've listened
to a thousand times, but couldn't hum a bar of?

In 1892, Alexander Berkman burst into Frick's
mansion and shot the steel baron. Frick
finished out the workday with his ledgers;
now his mansion is an art museum.
Berkman went to prison for 21 years, 7 in solitary.
When he came out, the world he'd known
had disappeared into smoke like a falling rocket.
How things bind and blend themselves together,
Ruskin cried out in the last paragraph he wrote.

father

riding the road
and the leaves falling
up and the words

slipping like charms onto a bracelet

what good is memory
1971 black ltd, smooth power steering—

—and the sun might have been gone
and the words might have been—

        and you?—

you too, riding
you too being unraveled like god

Praise Poem: June Jordan

Arms away, baby, the beautiful Bells Theorem's black!
We got bombed chicken, we got Chinese
chlorofluorocarbons. We gonna clean color
out of crazy Daddy Darkhead, out of his dedication to death.

DeLiza Dirt don't eminem her eyes.
Face it, father, flowers forget girls. Especially ones who got
head and heart. Here comes Indian laughter, here comes
Lebanon's light. Look!, I'm a mean momma, maybe

I'm a momma momma moon mother. My mouth
has always moved, especially when nobody have nothing.
A poet's racial profile is rain, river. Snow is a slim lady
or a somebody song. Stand in the streets.

Tell things to trees in Washington, DC.
Walk through the walls. Be a woman, be women.

Praise Poem: Muriel Rukeyser

Body. Breath.
The cloud colors. The child.
Dancing and dreaming the deep earth elegy,
you face the fathers, their fears, their flames. Fly greenly, girl,

hand yourself
to hills, to images of light, images of lives.
Lives who mountain the moon and moons
who never the nights. Know: peace surpasses poems and planes.

Remember rivers, shadows.
If they silence you into singing, sing sleep,
stars, stone, street—the things of this world.
Trees are turning into voices, waking women into waves.

Praise Poem: Jane Cooper

Sexual isn't a word she said six mornings a week. More likely
she'd be talking about teaching, birds, bomb tests, the threads
among them. I think she suffered like we all suffer
in wartime but poems were the rooms she walked into.
Alice said she was a pine, and sometimes I think
she got tangled in her own branches. Still,
everytime she let herself be an artist, went back
to writing, there were poems she'd already written,
and if not Muriel's speed of darkness,
they had the shine of silence.

Praise Poem: Edith Sitwell

You tasted furred apples from your bee-winged barouche
and with your motes and bells, you dusted the earth.
Some flames flowered, some glittering grew.
Your career, in contrast, is a nursery rhyme. For which
hambones and haycocks, with all their heart's honey,
don't give a jangle. To most, you're a dead o'er ondine,
a peaked polka queen with few repercussions. But
some of us, still wandering, find sheened soul
in your swan-bosomed velvet cream, and
whisper a waterfall for a witch who wore yellow.

Praise Poem: Emily Dickinson

To thee, thou,
unknown renown

our adamant fingers afraid and awakened

Praise Poem: Jan Heller Levi

She's the adopted daughter's version of an anatomy lesson,
the best friend of breasts and broken hearts. She wants
Eve-speaking eyes, and a Fall-River father
who's a friend to her music.

Her heart has been such an idiot.
She's the questions specific to rivers, she's
a slamming sleep under sticky
stars who's all about screaming
at the suburbs *shhh*

lo yang

lo yang

(1)

where is lo yang   where what can never be written
is written
just a few pages
just the dust of one hand

lo yang, i will give up all my possessions—

carved ivory ball within carved ivory ball,
small silver boatman
dipping his paddle in air,
two mothers
no fathers—

to find you

lo yang, you are the baby at my dream breast
even her
i will give up to find you

(2)

give me that wall

the wall you are carrying is very old and very heavy
let it go

no no
this is my wall

i love this wall

(3)

the root of bed is kin to *fodere*, to dig (a grave)
we dig a grave
our bed in the ground

we dig our bed, our bed in the ground
taste father dirt in our ears
mother ash in our eyes

        we don't long for words
        words don't long for their freedom from us

we read our stories in the dive of the narwhal
fluid industrious darkness
rising and descending in one motion

and in the marking of birds
illegible (if you're looking for straight lines)

(4)

small bridge, cold water

they are both clouds
their life is ten minutes

here we are, all drinking from a chalice
we blue virgins
we shepherds and sheep
we air singers
we wet footprints in the snow

we come to the edge and are lonely

do not be lonely
all this is our loneliness in its chalice

bright, wavering

(5)

collect enough paper
burn it

choose a bright lamp
turn it off

close the journal

let the buses chug, start, pass
let the heat knock its way up

little words inside   talk to each other   talk to
yourselves

(6)

my teacher's son asks, when is tomorrow?
he also says, they shouldn't call it a fire truck. it's a water truck

rain slashing slantwise across the window

"   "   "   "   "   "

the room breathes in anemones
breathes out her life

so let's call the bad dream the good dream

(7)

what do we see
what can we see without seeing
what have we been given
what has been taken away
what are the questions underneath our questions
how do we make our griefs our tools

(8)

sister, brother, don't you think

feeling itself, in this age of separations, may become a peculiar craft

(9)

the grass is drinking

the roses are drinking

the dark begins to unjoin from the light

the grass lies down, the sky gets on top
the roses open their mouths to drink the names of everything

you step forward
forward into one and two

forward into leaf touching leaf

NOTES

"That's the Way to Travel": For the story about what was done to the Romani in Europe, I am grateful to Colum McCann for his novel *Zoli*.

Please note also: The term "gypsy," which appears twice in the poem, is, of course, an exonym; it is what the Romani people were called by Europeans, not what they called themselves. When I use that word in the poem, I do so to underscore how such exonyms prevail in Western European and American culture; similar examples, among many, are the terms "cripple" (which I also use in the book), "invalid" (i.e. in-valid), and "handicapped" which emerges out of the identification of wounded veterans begging on the streets of London, with their "cap in hand."

"jane, staying" and "jane, staying (2)" are for Jane Cooper. "But I love this poor earth / because I have not seen another..." Jane used this line from Mandelstam as the epigraph for her poem, "Praise."

"One Little Thing": *Give me thy hand, my almost forgotten soul* is from Jung's *Red Book*. The original German is *Gib mir Deine Hand, meine fast vergessene Seele.*

"Praise Poem: June Jordan," "Praise Poem: Muriel Rukeyser," "Praise Poem: Jane Cooper," "Praise Poem: Edith Sitwell," "Praise Poem: Emily

Dickinson," and "Praise Poem: Jan Heller Levi": Google Books, at one time, provided a list of "frequently used words" in any particular book. These praise poems are composed of frequently used words, as Google identified them, of either collected poems, selected poems, or individual books, by June Jordan, Muriel Rukeyser, Jane Cooper, Edith Sitwell, Emily Dickinson, and myself. I took some liberties with order, and with connecting syntax, but not much. Let Google be used to praise poetry.

"lo yang": At the western gate of Lo Yang, in the 6th century B C, the Chinese sage Lao Tzu, before he left the city forever to end his days as a hermit in the forest, wrote his only text. He gave the pages to the gatekeeper, who had begged him to leave behind a book of his sacred teachings. That text, *The Tao* (The Way), begins—*The Tao that can be told is not the eternal Tao. / The name that cannot be named is not the eternal name*—thereby naming itself and erasing itself at the same time.

"*my teacher's son asks, when is tomorrow?*" is for Muriel Rukeyser.

"*sister, brother, don't you think...*": The last line in this poem is derived from a footnote in Karl Marx's *Capital*: "Ferguson had already said 1.c., p.281: 'And thinking itself, in this age of separations, may become a peculiar craft.'"

RECENT TITLES FROM ALICE JAMES BOOKS

Hum, Jamaal May
Viral, Suzanne Parker
We Come Elemental, Tamiko Beyer
Obscenely Yours, Angelo Nikolopoulos
Mezzanines, Matthew Olzmann
Lit from Inside: 40 Years of Poetry from Alice James Books, Edited by
    Anne Marie Macari and Carey Salerno
Black Crow Dress, Roxane Beth Johnson
Dark Elderberry Branch: Poems of Marina Tsvetaeva, A Reading by
    Ilya Kaminsky and Jean Valentine
Tantivy, Donald Revell
Murder Ballad, Jane Springer
Sudden Dog, Matthew Pennock
Western Practice, Stephen Motika
me and Nina, Monica A. Hand
Hagar Before the Occupation | Hagar After the Occupation,
    Amal al-Jubouri
Pier, Janine Oshiro
Heart First into the Forest, Stacy Gnall
This Strange Land, Shara McCallum
lie down too, Lesle Lewis
Panic, Laura McCullough
Milk Dress, Nicole Cooley
Parable of Hide and Seek, Chad Sweeney
Shahid Reads His Own Palm, Reginald Dwayne Betts
How to Catch a Falling Knife, Daniel Johnson
Phantom Noise, Brian Turner
Father Dirt, Mihaela Moscaliuc
Pageant, Joanna Fuhrman

ALICE JAMES BOOKS has been publishing poetry since 1973 and remains one of the few presses in the country that is run collectively. The cooperative selects manuscripts for publication primarily through regional and national annual competitions. Authors who win a Kinereth Gensler Award become active members of the cooperative board and participate in the editorial decisions of the press. The press, which historically has placed an emphasis on publishing women poets, was named for Alice James, sister of William and Henry, whose fine journal and gift for writing went unrecognized during her lifetime.

Designed by Dede Cummings
DCDESIGN

Printed by Thomson-Shore
on 30% postconsumer recycled paper
processed chlorine-free